FEAR

How To Overcome Following the Enemy's Advice Repeatedly

E. Renee Williams

LifePoint Publishing

Published by LifePoint Publishing Atlanta, Georgia

Printed in the USA. Cover Image © Fotolia

Library of Congress Control Number: 2012909286

ISBN: 978-0-9834460-0-2 (Paperback)

To my sons, I love you both dearly. I am thankful for my two precious gifts from the Lord.

Introduction

If you could choose to do anything and there were no limits to hold you back, what would you be able to do? What kind of difference would that make in your life? Fear imposes limits on the life of many individuals. You can choose not to be one of them. How has fear hindered you? Is there a dream you have that's been deferred or talents and gifts that have not been used? Take into consideration that promotion or new career, the business idea, continuing your education, a call into ministry, or the life of peace and confidence you've desired. Perhaps you have been blessed to accomplish many things, but still have a nagging feeling that you don't measure up or lost your sense of identity in the process. You may have faced various troubles and adversity in your life that has resulted in doubt, regret, rejection, or inadequacy. Whatever it may be, God has chosen you to glorify Him in it, to be an example or encouragement to others, and fulfill the purpose for your life.

Contents

1 Emotion and Spirit

There is one emotion that has the potential to cause destruction, wreck havoc, and keep you in bondage, that emotion is fear. When you allow fear to have control over your life, you continually experience dissatisfaction, regrets, and defeat.

Many people are driven by fear through an overwhelming level of insecurity, the fear of rejection influences their thinking and perception of how others think or feel. There is hope for healing the wounded heart.

Emotional Strongholds

Emotional strongholds occur when one is not effectively guarding their heart. Guarding our heart means that we are able to 'Hold on to that which is good', then identify and let go of things that are not conducive to a life of victory (Rom. 12:9).

Past hurts or significant events in life can lead you to feeling brokenhearted or disappointed over these things. This often gives way to fear and apprehension in certain areas of your life. However, you must understand that as a believer you are dealing with far more than just an emotion.

There is a spiritual battle that occurs in the life of a believer. "For God has not given us a spirit of fear, but of power and of love and of a sound mind (1 Tim. 1:7).

This scripture tells us that the spirit of fear is not from God. When you became a believer, the Holy Spirit came to reside within you full of power

2

and love that can only come from God. Your adversary, the devil seeks to steal, kill, and destroy. He will try to accomplish this in both the mind and emotions.

The enemy often works through the emotions as a way of discouraging and distracting you. It is important to know that there is nothing wrong with having a particular feeling or experiencing certain emotions, even fear.

However, the response that we have to these emotions is a determining factor of how they influence our lives. We must allow ourselves to feel in order to heal.

Once you come to terms with the issue of fear, you are able to face life head on knowing that God is your strength and He is able to carry you through your journey.

If there is ever anytime you are in need, you can certainly go to the Lord. He is our help, but unless you are honest with yourself and the Lord, you will continue to suffer in silence.

"So I remained utterly silent, not even saying anything good. But my anguish increased;" (Ps. 39:2 NIV).

You must not remain silent about your fear when you have a loving and powerful God that cares for you. There is freedom when your anxiety, insecurity, doubts, or inadequacy is cast upon Him. God's power is great enough to heal in the area of our emotions.

"The Lord is close to the brokenhearted; He rescues those whose spirits are crushed" (Ps. 34:18 NLT).

Clever Disguises

Just as the enemy is able to transform himself into an angel of light, so are the subtle snares and traps he uses to keep many in bondage come in disguise. The spirit of fear takes on varying forms that have the ability to impact every aspect of life if it is not recognized for what it actually is and dealt will properly.

Some of these forms can include feelings such as doubt, insecurity, inferiority, inadequacy, worry and apprehension. Although they may seem subtle, these feelings can be damaging to the daily life of the believer.

Insecurity and doubt can easily find its way into your life with the potential of keeping you from your divine purpose. As Moses encountered the burning bush, God chose him to lead his people out of Egypt.

Moses was insecure about himself and the mission that was set before him. At first he said, "Who am I that I should go to Pharaoh and bring the Israelites out of Egypt?" God assured Moses that He would be with him.

While Moses expressed his doubts about his lack of ability and fear of rejection, God promised to demonstrate His power through him (Exod. 3-4:17).

After the twelve spies gave the report about the giants in the land of Canaan, they became consumed by feelings of inferiority and inadequacy.

Despite the encouragement from Caleb, they said, "We seemed like grasshoppers in our own eyes, and we looked the same to them" (Num.13:33 NIV).

Martha experienced a sense of worry in the midst of serving. Jesus explained that the example Mary was setting of listening to Him was a better choice (Luke 10:38-42). Although fear is usually associated with panic, this emotion is also experienced as doubt, apprehension, insecurity, inadequacy, or inferiority.

At some point in time, everyone experiences fear in one form or another. Doubt often reveals itself as a sense of distrust or uncertainty. Many may suffer from feelings of insecurity or inadequacy, living without the courage needed to live out their purpose.

There are some people that feel inferior to others, either by their own perception or it could have been insinuated by the words or actions of someone else.

Fear in any of its forms can be a damaging emotion; if you give it the reigns, fear will determine the course of your life. When you choose to make decisions out of fear, it invites you to a place of bondage.

Being afraid to make a positive move to better yourself will leave you with regrets. Neglecting to live out the talents and dreams that God has given you can be heartbreaking.

There may always be the thought of, "If I had only finished that degree, changed careers, or started that business."

Many people have had dreams and goals that have been laying dormant deep within for such a long time. Perhaps you have been reluctant to move forward because you thought you did not have what it takes to get it accomplished. Believe and know that you can do all things through Christ that strengthen you (Phil. 4:13).

Effects of Fear

Fear is one of the most powerful tools in the enemy's arsenal of weapons against believers and those that have not accepted Christ. Many individuals have been bound by fear for so long that they cannot even imagine being free.

They have accepted fear-based thinking as a way of life. Some may even try to justify and excuse their negative thought life to keep from dealing with it effectively. When it comes down to it, there is often a lack of trust in God or an issue with pride. Both of which can lead to self-preservation and choosing a way that seems right to them and is not God's best for their life.

The effects of fear can have tremendous impact in various aspects of your life. Fear can cause you to live beneath your true potential, being afraid of success or hiding your talents.

You may become willing to endure disappointment than overcome fear. It may cause some people to take on the negative emotions or perceptions of others. Then there are times when fear will influence a person to please man rather than please God.

When you realize that God has destroyed the limits that keep you from maximizing your potential for His glory, you will have the courage needed to live a life of joy and peace. This courage will empower you to be all that God created you to become.

Fear

Fear impacts your mind by taking away your focus and the ability to use good judgment, which only leads to confusion and poor choices.

2 Schemes of the Devil

The devil is recognized by many names throughout scripture. His vile and deceitful nature has been documented in the Word of God. This adversary to the human race has and continues to make any attempt that he can to hinder the plan of God and discourage Christians from carrying out God's will(1 Thess.2:18). To be victorious in the Christian life we must learn to be vigilant, recognize, and respond effectively to the schemes of the devil. You must know the nature of your opponent and his strategy in order to win in spiritual warfare.

Satan's Origin

Prior to his fall and expulsion from heaven, Satan was an archangel, "an anointed cherub", before he tried to usurp the authority of God.

> You were the seal of perfection, full of wisdom and perfect in beauty. You were in Eden, the garden of God; every precious stone was you covering; the sardius, topaz, and diamond, beryl, onyx, and jasper, sapphire, turquoise, and emerald with gold. The workmanship of your timbrels and pipes was prepared for you on the day you were created. You were the anointed cherub who covers; I established you; you were on the holy mountain of God; you walked back and forth in the midst of fiery stones. You were perfect in your ways from the day you were created, til iniquity was found in you.

—Ezek.28:13-15

He became greatly inflated with pride.

How you are fallen from heaven O' Lucifer, son of the morning! How you are cut down to the ground, you who weakened the nations! For you have said in your heart: 'I will ascend into heaven, I will exalt my throne above the stars of God; I will also sit on the mount of the congregation on the farthest sides of the north; I will ascend above the heights of the clouds, I will be like the Most High.' Yet you shall be brought down to Sheol, to the lowest depths of the Pit.

—Isaiah 14:12-15

He was consumed by his splendor. Satan was a created being who deceived himself into thinking that he could possibly exalt himself to be like God. In his rebellion, he enlisted a third of the angels (Rev. 12:4).

This sin resulted in him being cast out of heaven because he desired to be equal with God (Luke 10:18). He proved himself to be the originator of sin.

Character of Satan

Many verses of scripture reveal his nature and how he operates. He is the tempter that came to Jesus after forty days of fasting to test him (Matt. 4:3). He is the accuser of those that trust in the Lord (Rev.12:10) and blinds the minds of unbelievers to keep them from believing the gospel (2 Cor. 4:4). The book of Revelation tells us that he is the one that deceives the whole world (Rev. 12:9).

Since he was cast down from heaven for his sin of pride and rebellion, he is considered the, "Prince of this world", or rather the world system (John 12:31). This is considered a system of values, ideas, and activities that are opposed to the plan of God. The enemy is declared a thief, murderer, and destroyer of what gives God glory (John 8:44)

In the Garden

The book of Genesis gives the account of what took place in the Garden of Eden. It is here where we see one of the many ways in which the enemy operates.

> Now the serpent was more cunning than any beast of the field which the Lord God had made. And he said to the Woman, "Has God indeed said, 'you shall not eat of every tree of the garden'?" And the woman said to the serpent, "We may eat the fruit of the trees of the garden; but of the fruit of the tree which is in the midst of the garden, God has said, "You shall not eat it, nor shall you touch it, lest you die'" Then the serpent said to the woman, "You will not surely die. For God knows that in the day you eat of it your eyes will be opened, and you will be like God, knowing good and evil." So when the woman saw that the tree was good for food, that it was pleasant to the eyes and a tree desirable to make one wise, she took of its fruit and ate. She also gave to her husband with her, and he ate. Then the eyes of both of them were opened,

and they knew that they were naked, and
they sewed fig leaves together and made
themselves covering.

—Gen. 3:1-7

In this passage we see how the enemy, in the
form of a serpent, uses doubt to tempt and deceive. He posed a question to Eve that put empha-
sis only on part of what God actually said,

"And the Lord God commanded the man, saying, "Of every tree of the garden you may freely
eat, but of the tree of the knowledge of good and
evil you shall not eat, for in the day that you eat of
it you shall surely die"(Gen.2:16).

He presented the lie to her that they would not
die. The enemy then insinuated a sense of mis-
trust that God may have been holding back on
Adam and Eve something to be desired. The truth
is they were already created in the image of God
(Gen. 1:27). Satan was baiting them to follow the
same fatal path that he chose in his former state

as Lucifer—seeking equality with God (Isa. 14:14).

The enemy knew if he could get them to sin that their disobedience would lead to guilt, shame, condemnation, and fear. It also affected their relationship to God and their identity. In verse seven "their eyes were opened."

This certainly does not mean they were walking around with their eyes closed or without sight. When their eyes were opened they began to perceive themselves in a negative way. This verse also states, "they knew that they were naked." Prior to their disobedience they were "naked and not ashamed" (Gen. 2:25). They experienced guilt before God. Their relationship with God was changed and their sins separated them from the fellowship they once knew.

"So he said, "I heard Your voice in the garden, and I was afraid because I was naked; and I hid myself."(Gen. 3:10).

Fear

Adam and Eve's decision to follow the enemy's advice instead of believing and trusting in God resulted in fear and shame. You must not allow yourself to entertain thoughts of doubt or fear that the enemy projects.

3 Bondage to Fear

The enemy takes great pleasure in a believer that is bound by fear. If he can get you to be held captive by fear, then he can succeed in keeping you from experiencing a meaningful relationship with the Lord. Fear, insecurity, doubt and inadequacy will begin to take ownership of a person, as children of God we must understand and embrace the reality of our acceptance into the family of God through Jesus Christ. Although we have the assurance of salvation the moment we accepted Jesus as our Lord and Savior, there may still be a struggle with the emotions that resulted from experiences of our old life and through our spiritual growth in the Lord.

Even though we are no longer subject to the power of sin and death, Satan will try to capitalize on those negative emotions, bringing the believer into bondage. He uses past sins, shame, and rejection from people as a means of entrapment.

Pain of the Past

The devil attempts to bring you into remembrance of your past, ultimately his goal is to make you feel like a victim instead of a victor. Through these tactics he manages to divert our focus from the foundational truths of the gospel (2 Cor. 11:3).

"For God made Christ, who never sinned, to be the offering for our sin, so that we could be made right with God through Christ." (2 Cor. 5:21 NLT)

We are better equipped to stand against the schemes of the devil when we internalize the truth about where we stand with God. Too often, many Christians get stuck in a mode of defeat from issues of the past. This can cause an individual to become enslaved to the hurts and mistakes that God has long ago forgotten.

"Forget the former things; do not dwell on the past. See, I am doing a new thing Now it springs up; do you not perceive it? I am making a way in the desert and streams in the wasteland" (Isa. 43:18-19 NIV)

In the same manner that He commanded the Israelites to forget the bondage they experienced to Babylon, we too must not dwell on the bondage of our past. We do not have to be subject to the things that have caused us to be in fear, we have to stop and ask ourselves, "Am I truly aware of what took place in my life when I accepted Jesus?" To live in victory it is imperative that we actualize what God has done for us through His son Jesus. It is not enough for us to simply go to church week in and week out and get into a spiritualized routine. We may know scripture backwards and forwards or even serve within the church and community, but we must go beyond routine and a head-knowledge into a heart-knowledge. This is achieved by spending time in His presence through prayer, meditating on the Word, and applying its principles to our lives daily.

Many well meaning Christians may say that we must be able to forgive ourselves for the mistakes that were made in the past in order to move on from them. However, what we are actually doing in a sense is diminishing the forgiving power of God and the atoning work of Christ.

This is actually adapting to the world's philosophy of "fixing it" ourselves. We must remember that those who are in the world are blinded by the enemy and do not believe they are accountable to God (2 Cor. 4:4). And therefore do not understand the need of His forgiveness. They believe that they can handle things on their own. As believers, we should not adapt our thinking to the way the world thinks.

"And we have such trust through Christ toward God. Not that we are sufficient of ourselves to think of anything as being from ourselves, but our sufficiency is from God" (2 Cor.3:4-5).

As Christians, we must resist the temptation towards a perception of self-forgiveness. In doing so we are exalting or own ability above God's power and authority in our lives. By requiring our own forgiveness in addition to forgiveness of God, this leads us to being held captive by the things we have done.

This causes us to never be truly able to get beyond those past experiences, placing us in a vicious cycle of resentment and self-condemnation. Instead of embracing what God's word has declared to us and accepting the reality of His forgiveness, we end up in a perpetual frame of mind that is influenced by the enemy. This is precisely what Satan desires and is consistent with his nature as the accuser of those who love the Lord (Rev. 12:10).

The enemy wants nothing more than for a believer to be held captive by the notion that they are lacking in forgiveness from God concerning a particular aspect or situation in their life. By impressing the idea of self-forgiveness upon us he cripples the ability to fully embrace and comprehend our redemption from the bondage to fear.

> When He saw their faith, He said to him, "Man, your sins are forgiven you." And the scribes and the Pharisees began to reason, saying, "Who is this who speaks blasphemies? Who can forgive sins but God alone?" But when Jesus perceived their thoughts, He answered and said to them, "Why are you reasoning in your hearts? Which is easier, to say, 'Your sins are forgiven you,' or to say, 'Rise up and walk'? But that you may know that the Son of Man has power on earth to forgive

sins" He said to the man who was paralyzed, "I say to you, arise, take up your bed, and go to your house."

—Luke 5:20-24

The Pharisees were aware that only God can forgive sin, but they failed to recognize the fullness of deity in Christ and that He is the very One with the power to forgive sins. They refused to accept the power that Jesus has to forgive. In the same manner that the paralytic received physical healing, we can experience spiritual healing when we realize that all our sins have been forgiven. There are no other prerequisites to walking in freedom than to believe that Jesus came to die for your sin, repent and to confess Him as Lord of your life (Rom. 10:9).

Condemnation

Being in bondage to fear can lead to self-condemnation. Self-condemnation makes a person feel as if they cannot forgive themselves for mistakes or poor decisions of the past.

The enemy leads you into bondage and the fear that something you have done in the past is somehow unforgiveable by God. This impresses upon you the notion that there is something you have to do in order to get over what happened. Satan deceives us into thinking that it is possible for us to obtain forgiveness through ourselves. He gains an advantage by diminishing the power of the Cross and Jesus' sacrifice for us by the rehearsal of past hurts and sins in the mind.

This causes many Christians to beat themselves up over things that happened years, even decades ago, leading to bitterness that will torment not only them but also those around them. It could be due to sin in their own life or the weight of false guilt from sin that was acted upon them by others through various forms of abuse.

Through this subtle and crafty scheme, the enemy leads us into deception and away from the simplicity of the Gospel (2Cor. 11:3). In doing so, it places the believer into bondage to the fear that they are not able to move beyond the events that took place.

Some may say, "I know Jesus died for my sins and I have been forgiven, but I just don't feel forgiven." Actually, this plays right into the enemy's plan to cause us to be so entangled by our emotions that we are lured away from the foundational truth of the gospel.

Our feelings have no bearing on the reality of the forgiveness we have received through Christ. "Even if we feel guilty, God is greater than our feelings, and he knows everything." (1 John 3:20 NLT). He knows that you have accepted His Son as your Lord and Savior. He knows that the death on the cross was the only way to reconcile mankind to Himself. He knows there is nothing you can do to accomplish this for yourself.

Fear of Man

The fear of man can make the life of a Christian ineffective and unfruitful. "The fear of man brings a snare, but whoever trust in the Lord will be safe" (Prov. 29:25). The fear of man can also cause you to not live out what you truly believe because of what people might say or think. Your relationship with God will only end up taking a backseat, and the desire to please man will dominate your life. You may also find yourself adjusting your behavior in order to be accepted or impress others.

> But when Peter came to Antioch, I had to oppose him to his face, for what he did was very wrong. When he first arrived, he ate with the Gentile Christians, who were not circumcised. But afterward, when some friends of James

came, Peter wouldn't eat with the Gentiles anymore, He was afraid of criticism from these people who insisted on the necessity of circumcision.

—Gal. 2:11-12 NLT

Christians that have a fear of man are more likely to compromise in situations that are not consistent with the principles of God's precious word. A person may be afraid of what other people might say or do in regards to a decision or action. Some are even afraid to fully live out their lives in honor of God, because they do not want to experience the rejection of people close to them.

"Yet at the same time many even among the leaders believed in him. But because of the Pharisees they would not openly acknowledge their faith for fear they would be put out of the synagogue; for they loved human praise more than praise from God." (John 12:42-43 NIV)

In fact, you should not be surprised, but you are considered blessed if you are insulted because of the name of Christ. "God blesses you when people mock you and persecute you and lie about you and say all sorts of evil things against you because you are my followers" (Matt. 5:11 NLT).

Being overly dependent upon the opinions of others can lead to fear. The enemy often uses people as a way to discourage you. It is usually easier to let go of an insult or hurtful remark by a stranger. However, when it comes from someone you love or respect it can hurt even more. Satan knows this, so he will use people that you are close to or interact with regularly as a way to hinder you from your purpose in Christ.

People often try to project their own fears onto you. Sometimes it is through snide remarks or veiled comments. They might also try to use intimidation or downplay your goals or successes. Some may even go so far as to defame your character and try to discredit you. This is usually done in an effort to feel better about themselves and cover for their own mistakes or insecurities. Instead of dealing with their own fears, it's easier to be critical or malevolent towards others.

You must remember that God sees all; He knows the thoughts of the mind and the intentions of the heart of mankind. It is our responsibility to trust in Him and take Him at His word. The bible tells us "No weapon forged against you will prevail, and you will refute every tongue that accuses you. This is the heritage of the servants of the Lord, and this is their vindication from Me, declares the Lord" (Isa. 54:17 NIV).

You are loved so dearly by God. He has accepted you as His own. As His precious child, you no longer have to live with the fear of rejection. You have the acceptance and approval of God. You don't have to fear man or be preoccupied with pleasing everyone around you. The Psalmist makes it clear, "In God, whose word I praise, in God I trust; I will not be afraid. What can mortal man do to me?" (Ps.56:4 NIV).

4 Identity Theft

Understanding who we are in Christ is essential if we are to live the Christian life successfully. When we allow fear to dominate our lives, it is evident that we are not operating in the identity we were given at our rebirth in Christ. The enemy wants to convince us that we are any and everything except for what God's word has said about us. His desire is to rob us of the assurance and confidence that comes from being in a relationship in Christ. "The thief comes only to steal and kill and destroy; I have come that they may have life, and have it to the full" (John 10:10 NIV).The devil is on a mission to diminish your sense of value and worth in order to keep you from focusing on the things of God. In addition to eternal life, Jesus also came so we may experience and enjoy a meaningful life here and now that glorifies God; a life of significance that is centered on the truth of God's word and His love.

Satan's Mission to Deceive

The enemy tries to hijack your identity by insinuating that you are not all that God's Word has declared you to be. He understands that if he can keep a Christian from operating in their divine capacity, he can continue to keep them in bondage to fear, doubt, shame, and guilt.

When you allow the enemy to get into your mind, he asserts ideas of doubt regarding your identity in Christ. We have a Savior that can relate to the way we are tempted by the enemy

(Heb 4:15). In Luke 4:3-4, Satan attacks the identity of Jesus:

And the devil said to Him, "If You are the Son of God, command this stone to become bread." But Jesus answered him, saying, "It is written, 'Man shall not live by bread alone, but by every word of God.' "

In that moment, the enemy disregarded the truth about who Christ was in a failed attempt to thwart Him from the purpose He was destined to fulfill. As believers, we encounter the same type of attacks that are intended to get us to doubt our identity in Christ. Just as Jesus countered this move of the enemy, we too must depend on the Word of God to sustain us. The enemy will try to convince you that you're not good enough, didn't come from the right family, have the right education, title, or own the best material things. He will use people in your life—in many cases those that are the closest to you—as a tool to administer discouragement and project negative ideas that are in contradiction to what God's word says. We must not allow ourselves to be deceived by the enemy's schemes.

We read in the book of Zechariah how the enemy attempts to make his accusations before the Lord:

> Then the angel showed me Jeshua the high priest standing before the angel of the Lord. The Accuser, Satan, was there at the angel's right hand, making accusations against Jeshua. And the Lord said to Satan, "I, the Lord, reject your accusations, Satan. Yes, the Lord, who has chosen Jerusalem, rebukes you. This man is like a burning stick that has been snatched from the fire." Jeshua's clothing was filthy as he stood there before the angel. So the angel said to the others standing there, "Take off his filthy clothes." And turning to Jeshua he said, "See I have taken away your sins, and now I am giving you these fine

new clothes" Then I said, "They should also place a clean turban on his head." So they put a clean priestly turban on his head and dressed him in new clothes while the angel of the Lord stood by.

—Zech. 3:1-5 NLT

Since the Lord rejects the lies of the devil, how much more then are you to be able to reject these same lies as children of God? You have the power of the Holy Spirit dwelling in you (1 Cor. 6:19). And this power is far greater than any scheme the enemy may try to pull (1 John 4:4).

Every lie and accusation of the enemy is erroneous and irrelevant. Every believer is part of a royal priesthood (1 Pet. 2:9). Therefore, it is essential that we be mindful of the fact that our filthy garments have been replaced with a robe of righteousness through faith in Jesus Christ (Isa. 61:10, Rom. 3:22).

Reclaiming Your Identity

If you are to overcome fear, doubt, or insecurity, you need to believe what the word of God says about you. Having a clear understanding of what took place when you were born again is essential to living with confidence. We are only able to operate based on what we believe to be true about ourselves. One of the worst things we can do is to approach God's word with a mindset of defeat, only focusing on everything we are not, instead of believing all that we are in Christ. Let's take a look at the book of Colossians:

> When you came to Christ, you were "circumcised," but not by a physical procedure. Christ performed a spiritual circumcision—the cutting away of your sinful nature. For you were buried with Christ when you were baptized. And with him you were raised to new life because you trusted the mighty power of God,

who raised Christ from the dead.

—Col. 2:11-12 NLT

The enemy wants to distract us from the truth about the new nature we received and persuade us to dwell on what we were before accepting Christ, and the things done after the new birth. This keeps us from functioning based on our new identity because once we truly realize who we are in Christ and the level of power we posses, we become an imminent danger to Satan and his fallen angels.

Recognize the enemy for the fraud that he is and the father of lies. Counter every feeling of doubt, insecurity, or fear with God's greatness. Rejoice and meditate on all the ways God has been good to you. Consider the areas in which you have been vulnerable or hurt, and let the promises of God be your anchor. Go to the Lord in prayer, reveal to Him your hurts, pain, and cast all your cares upon Him.

Anti-theft Protection

Many individuals go out of there way to protect their homes, cars, and personal belongings from intruders and those that seek to destroy and take what does not belong to them. In this same manner, we as Christians must have the same sense of urgency in protecting what is rightfully ours through Christ. Our identity in Him is more precious than any material thing we have, it is the result of the new life we found in Jesus. The enemy does not want you to be secure in who you are, especially your life in Christ. We must protect ourselves through the power of the Holy Spirit and stand on the truth of God's word.

"There is therefore now no condemnation to those who are in Christ Jesus, who do not walk according to the flesh, but according to the Spirit" (Rom. 8:1). Since you are in relationship with Christ, there is no longer a reason to feel inadequate, rejected, shame, guilt, defeat, uncertainty, or fear. The key to achieving this is walking according to the Spirit and being dependent upon Him leading, guiding, and comforting us along the way. We can not acquire a sense of security through the works of the flesh. No matter what we do, even if we are doing "all the right things"— but not trusting the Lord to protect and keep us— we can invite condemnation. That's why it is crucial for us to rest in His power and grace.

It is such a joy to know that there is absolutely nothing and no one that can stand against the work of Jesus Christ. "For God made Christ, who never sinned, to be the offering for our sin, so that we could be made right with God through Christ" (2 Cor. 5:21 NLT). The sinless life of Jesus was the substitution for the penalty of our sin. His sacrifice on the cross made us right with God and enabled us to be in relationship with Him when we confessed our sin and accepted Jesus as our savior.

"This righteousness from God comes through faith in Jesus Christ to all who believe. There is no difference, for all have sinned and fall short of the glory of God" (Rom. 3:22-23 NIV). You were not declared righteous because of anything that you have done. You may have an active prayer life, study the bible regularly, give tithe and offering, participate in ministry or the community, and faithful in church attendance.

All of these things are products of the Christian life, but merely doing them without true relationship leaves you empty. Righteousness is the result of a loving relationship with God, through faith in Jesus Christ. Having the assurance of your salvation is key to dealing with the negativity the enemy tries to throw your way. Since you are in Christ, there is no need to allow yourself to continue to carry feelings of guilt, shame, insecurity, or condemnation (Rom. 8:1)

What shall we say about such wonderful things as these? If God is for us, who can ever be against us? Since He did not spare even his own Son but gave him up for us all, won't He, also give us everything else? Who dares accuse us whom God has chosen for His own? No one—for God Himself has given us right standing with Himself. Who then will condemn us? No one—for Christ Jesus died for us and was raised to life for us and He is sitting in the place of honor at God's, right hand pleading for us.

—Romans 8:31-34

In Jesus we have an advocate that is continually pleading for us against every accusation of the devil or anyone he uses to discourage us. You must remember that we are to lead fruitful lives free from habitual sin and above reproach. Lives lived carnally gives the devil the ammunition he needs to heap condemnation upon us and maintain the bondage to fear. Live a life that is led by the Spirit and not your emotions.

Although we are not to purposely live a sinful life, we are still living in fleshly bodies. We do not have to be subject to the flesh and can choose to walk in the Spirit. If we do sin we have the assurance that Christ is at our defense (1 John 2:1), and we can continue in righteousness (1 John 1:9).

Regardless of the accusations directed towards us, God has canceled the charges against us at the cross (Col. 2:14). "Because God's children are human beings— made of flesh and blood— Jesus also became flesh and blood by being born in human form. For only as a human being could he die, and only by dying could he break the power of the devil, who had the power of death"(Heb. 2:14 NLT). The enemy no longer has any claim on us because we are children of God, nor does he have any power over us because of the death of Jesus Christ.

5 Examining Ourselves

Although the devil is busy roaming about, there is still a need for self-examination. At times, as a fallen people, we can get in our own way—becoming our own worst enemy. It is essential that you take a look within to determine where the enemy's attacks end and our personal responsibility begins.

Self-Examination

The apostle Paul gave advice and posed a question to the Corinthians, "Examine yourselves as to whether you are in the faith. Test yourselves. Do you not know yourselves that Jesus Christ is in you?" (2 Cor. 13:5). This was a very important point the Apostle made.

Despite the flaming arrows that are hurled at you by the enemy, you must also consider your life 'in the faith'. Is the faith you have from a genuine relationship with the Lord or is it based on religious performance?

Are you more fearful of what others think or if you are considered to be a "good Christian"? Are you living a life that is driven by the strength that Christ gives or still trying to make it on your own terms? These are some of the things that need to be examined. Understanding that you have the Holy Spirit dwelling inside to strengthen and give you the ability to live through God's awesome power.

He also gives you the courage to examine yourself for any hindrance in your life. This can include any type of sin. Unconfessed sin or issues that have not been properly dealt with can contribute to the feelings associated with fear like doubt, insecurity, and apprehension.

When you confess your sins to the Lord you experience freedom, because He will forgive you and cleanse you from them (1 John 1:9).

Stripping away the things that hinder you will allow you to enjoy the Christian life as God intended—a life of joy, peace, and contentment. Addressing the weights or hindrances that impede is not always easy.

However, it is necessary if you desire a life that is not based on fear.

> We think you ought to know, dear brothers and sisters, about the trouble we went through in the province of Asia. We were crushed and overwhelmed beyond our ability to endure, and we thought we would never live through it. In fact, we expected to die. But as a result, we stopped relying on our-

selves and learned to rely only on God, who
raises the dead.

—2 Cor. 1:8-9 NLT

Paul explained the devastating effects the
hardships experienced in his ministry impacted
him and his fellow laborers in the gospel. He
understood that he was not to be dependent soley
on human effort, but to rely on God. You do not
have to worry about living a life performing out of
the expectations of others. You also don't have to
live life on your own terms, but in dependence on
God. The Lord will guide you as you look within.

"Behold you desire truth in the inner parts;
and in the hidden part you will make me to know
wisdom" (Psalm 51:6 NIV). Being honest with
yourself and God is a crucial step in letting go of
fear.

Heart of the Matter

As you take a closer look at fear and how it has
the potential to impact the life of a believer, it is

easy to see that humility is needed for victory. At the very core of fear is an underlying issue of pride.

Although we may not always recognize it, pride is what keeps a believer from being dependent on the strength God gives. You must understand that the Lord is near and ready for you to relinquish your fears and be confident in his, ability to care for you.

Pride is what causes a person to lean on their own understanding instead of seeking the Lord for direction. When a person is entangled by fear, it makes them reluctant to let go of negative emotions and often leads them to seek their own path in life.

Pride leads to self-preservation. The bible tells us that it is foolish to trust in ourselves and better to operate out of wisdom (Prov. 28:26). There is nothing of ourselves that can provide more protection or assurance than the love of God.

Fear

"There is no fear in love. But perfect love drives out fear, because fear has to do with punishment. The one who fears is not made perfect in love" (1 John 4:18 NIV).

Have you truly allowed the perfect love of God to permeate your mind and heart? When you have fully experienced God's perfect love it dispels doubt, insecurity, or any other experience associated with fear.

The fullness of His love gives you freedom and relationship with Him. Without His perfect love to complete you, the torment and emotional distress will leave you feeling incomplete and full of doubt.

Guarding the Heart

In examining yourself, it is important to keep watch over your heart. Many have referred to the heart as the seat of the emotions.

This means that it is absolutely necessary for a believer to be alert, especially in regards to feelings that develop out of fear.

"Above all else, guard your heart, for everything you do flows from it" (Prov. 4:23 NIV).

When guarding the heart, it is important to watch what flows out and what you allow inside. The enemy may try to do what he can to fill your heart with negativity.

However, it is up to you when examining yourself to manage the propensities of the heart effectively. There are many bad things that can flow out of the heart, but it is up to you to deposit good things in the heart.

As a believer, you must hide God's Word in your heart (Psalm 119:11). This will be your best defense in guarding your heart. Moreover, allow the peace of God to keep your heart (Phil. 4:7).

It is His peace that will help you to be diligent in guarding your heart, because you know the truth of His Word and holding fast to His promises can dispel fear.

6 Trusting the Lord

Trusting in the Lord takes faith. Trying to live the Christian life without it is like attempting to drive a vehicle running on empty. Fear has a way of taking such a strong hold upon many individuals that it may be hard to envision themselves with the joy and peace they've previously known. This does not have to be the case for you.

Faith vs. Fear

The emotions related to fear can be draining and impact your level of trust in the Lord.

Fear

"Now faith is the substance of things hoped for, the evidence of things not seen." (Heb. 11:1)

Faith is what gives you confidence and the assurance that God is all powerful and able to do as His Word has promised. You may not know the end of a situation and how it may turn out, but you can be certain that God will work things out according to His perfect will.

The enemy uses fear through doubt and uncertainty to keep you from focusing on the promises of God. The devil knows that if he can cause you to wavier in your faith, then you will be the perfect target for his destruction.

A spirit of fear in the life of a believer is a clear indication of a deficiency of trust in the Lord. Throughout the scriptures He has shown Himself to be faithful time after time. He has promised to be with you always (Matt. 28:20).

Fear of the Lord

To fear the Lord does not mean that you are gripped by panic because of Him. It is reverence and awe for His power, wisdom, and presence. It is the beginning of wisdom for those that love Him (Prov. 9:10).

When we submit ourselves to the power of God, He will lift us up and give us the strength to do more than we can ever imagine or ask of Him (Eph. 3:20). To experience peace we must yield to the fact that God is in control and knows exactly how to deliver us from our afflictions. "Therefore submit to God. Resist the devil and he will flee from you." (James 4:7).

Our ability to resist the devil is based on our willingness to submit to God. We submit to God by having complete and unwavering faith in Him. "Without faith it is impossible to please God (Heb. 11:6). There are times when the Lord will test us to reveal where our hearts are and bring us to a place of dependence upon Him. The children of Israel experienced this first hand in the wilderness when they complained against God and Moses:

> And the people spoke against Moses; "Why have you brought us up out of Egypt to die in the wilderness? For there is no food and no water, and our soul loathes this worthless bread." So the Lord sent fiery serpents among the people, and they bit the people; and many of the people of Israel died. Therefore the people came to Moses, and said, "We have sinned, for we have spoken against the Lord and against you; pray to the Lord that He take away the serpents from us." So Moses prayed for the people. Then the Lord said to Moses, "Make a fiery serpent, and set it on a pole; and it shall be that everyone who is bitten, when he looks at it, shall live." So Moses made a bronze serpent, and put it on a pole and so it was, if a serpent had bitten anyone,

when he looked at the bronze serpent, he
lived.

—Num.21:5-9

As we take a closer look at verse six, we notice
that the people wanted the Lord to "take away the
serpents". Often, when we are going through
troubles there is a tendency to question God about
why we have to endure undesirable circumstances. Like the people of Israel, we wonder, "Why me
Lord?" When Moses prayed, the Lord commanded
him to make an image of the very thing that
caused them so much anguish.

The purpose of them looking at the bronze serpent was to get them to a point where they were
willing to face their pain and depend on God.
When we face the issues that cause us to be
discouraged or even threaten our well being we
are given an opportunity to live. Once it is understood that the trials and tribulations we are faced
with are only a test that God has permitted for

our good (Deut. 8:16), we begin to comprehend the sovereignty and grace of the God we serve. Trials are inevitable. However, we must understand that we are not in this alone and that we do not have to tackle these issues in our own strength. Place your trust in Him for the strength to endure.

Trusting Through Adversity

Being a Christian does not mean that you will never experience trials or adversity. In fact, the Bible tells us not to be surprised when we do encounter them (1 Pet. 4:12). Everyone will face same type of trial or adversity at some point in their life. The demands and events that you encounter can impact you to the point that you are having feelings of uncertainty and apprehension about many things.

You can be sure that God is aware of your troubles and is able to strengthen you during difficult times. Satan uses fear as a way to paralyze or frustrate a believer in an effort to wear down confidence. God's word gives you assurance that He will be with you. "Fear not, for I am with you; be not dismayed, for I am your God. I will strengthen you, yes, I will help you, I will uphold you with My righteous right hand" (Isa. 41:10)

The enemy often uses other people in your life who may try to discourage you or invoke fear by saying or doing hurtful things. But the scriptures are clear about handling this, "In God I have put my trust, I will not be afraid. What can man do to me?" (Ps. 56:11).

Regardless of the type of adversity you face, believe that God is in complete control and He knows what is best for your life. "And we know that in all things God works for the good of those who love Him, who have been called according to His purpose" (Rom. 8:28 NIV). You do not have to allow yourself to be overwhelmed and succumb to the pressures and trials that you face. We serve an all powerful and mighty God; He alone knows exactly how to deliver you out of trouble.

He can use the difficulties you face to bring you into a closer and more intimate relationship with Him. The time of adversity in your life is not an indication that you are less of a Christian or that you don't have your life together.

This is a lie from the enemy, because you have been made whole and complete through Christ. Other people may look at your struggle and are not aware that God may be using those unfortunate challenges as a way to accomplish His perfect will. Don't worry if some of the people in your life scoff at you or may not understand God's sovereignty.

7 Engaging in Battle

In order for you to win the spiritual battle in your life you must understand the nature of your opponent and know exactly what you are dealing with as a Christian. Satan wages a war against the mind of a believer. His desire is to thwart you from God's purpose. Therefore, it is essential that you are equipped for spiritual warfare.

Recognizing Your Opponent

The first epistle of Peter makes it clear: "Be sober, be vigilant; because your adversary the devil walks about like a roaring lion seeking whom he may devour. Resist him, steadfast in the faith (1 Pet. 5:8-9a). These verses let you know that the enemy is constantly roaming about looking for someone on whom he can project his lies. It is important that your mind is free from fear-based thinking.

All believers need to stay alert; this in no way means that you have to constantly be preoccupied with the threats of the enemy. It simply means that you need to be able to recognize his schemes and learn how to counter them with truth (2 Cor. 2:11).

The enemy works through your emotions by inserting doubt and uncertainty. His mission is to deceive and keep you from understanding the truth of God's Word and accepting it as your reality (Mark 4:15).

The enemy would much rather see you in bondage to fear than experiencing the freedom that was given to you the day you accepted Jesus as your Savior. It is up to you to accept the truth of God's Word and not follow the advice of the enemy's lies. Believe the truth of scripture when it says:

"God has not given us a spirit of fear, but of power and of love and of a sound mind" (2 Tim. 1:7).

You have been empowered and equipped to win your spiritual battles. Jesus himself declared that He has given you power over the enemy (Luke 10:19).

When you know that your thoughts have drifted to a negative experience or something that evokes fear, you can shut it down by going to God's word and meditating on verses related to your situation.

God's word is powerful and will give you the strength to deal with your circumstances.

Battle of the Mind

As a believer, there will be moments when you will encounter a spiritual battle. The battleground is the mind, were the enemy makes his accusations and insinuations that conflict the truth of God's Word.

> Put on the whole armor of God that you may be able to stand against the wiles of the devil. For we do not wrestle against flesh and blood, but against principalities, against powers, against the rulers of the darkness of this age, against spiritual hosts of wickedness in the heavenly places.
>
> —Eph. 6:11-12

We are not in a war that we can see, yet the impact on our spiritual lives are very real. Although Satan may work through others and influence them to act on his behalf, he is a spirit being (Matt. 16:23). You have been given power through the righteousness and authority of Jesus Christ.

Engaging in Battle

The weapons issued to you for battle are designed to demolish the attacks of the enemy.

> For though we walk in the flesh, we do not war according to the flesh. For the weapons of our warfare are not carnal but mighty in God for the pulling down of strongholds, casting down arguments and every high thing that exalts itself against the knowledge of God, bringing every thought into captivity in the obedience of Christ, and being ready to punish all disobedience when your obedience is fulfilled.
>
> —2 Cor. 10:3-5

You may deal with similar struggles as the world, yet the manner by which you deal with them is through the power of an awesome God. You no longer have to fight your battles as the world does, depending solely on themselves and human understanding.

Through the weapons that God gives you are able to break free of the strongholds that the enemy has used to ensnare many believers. The "what ifs" or speculations about life only fuels fear and keeps you in bondage.

When the enemy tries to insert doubt, fear, inferiority, or uncertainty into your mind, you have the power to destroy the arguments and cast down anything that contradicts God's Word. You can take every thought captive and filter it through the truth of God's word. It is essential that you make time to study your bible, so you may understand and know the truth. Examining your thought-life through the truth of scripture will allow you to discern between the lies from the enemy and God's promise.

You must refuse to accept the wrong perceptions and negative thoughts that the enemy presents to you. To do this you need God's armor:

Therefore take up the whole armor of God, that you may be able to withstand in the evil day, and having done all, stand. Stand therefore, having girded you waist with truth, having put on the breastplate of righteousness, and having shod your feet with the preparation of the gospel of peace; above all, taking the shield of faith with which you will be able to quench all the fiery darts of the wicked one. And take the helmet of salvation; and the sword of the Spirit; which is the word of God.

—Eph. 6:13-17

The greatest weapon in our arsenal against Satan is truth. God's truth dispels every lie and deception of the enemy. The breastplate of righteousness protects you when you clothe yourself in the righteousness of Christ. It is through Him that we have been made right with God.

You are able to stand firm on the foundation of the gospel. Faith is what extinguishes the fiery darts of doubt and uncertainty. When you believe that what God says is true, the enemy can no longer use fear to keep you in bondage.

The helmet of salvation causes you to be mindful of the assurance of your salvation. You don't have to question your relationship with the Lord. Another crucial weapon is the Word of God. It holds the answer to every doubt and speculation that conflicts what God says.

Renewing the Mind

By neglecting to renew the mind you will continually find yourself plagued with the same struggles throughout the course of life. We must not base our lives on our emotions and what we feel, but on the truth that is in the Word of God. The enemy is depending on you being held captive by your emotions.

This places you in the perfect position by which he can wreck havoc on your life and keep you from realizing the greatness that is within you.

As your mind is renewed, you must decide not to respond to the issues of life in the same manner as the world or present culture. You need to let go of the negative thought patterns. It is not enough to have the right weapons, but you must also know how to use them.

It is imperative that your mind is renewed from the lies of the enemy and wrong perceptions. Having a wrong mindset is referred to in scripture as being carnally-minded (Rom. 8:6). Being carnally minded results in spiritual death. It is a loss of intimacy and sense of connection to God. The carnal mind focuses more on things of the flesh. In other words, living life based on what is right in your own eyes; your perception is distorted by fear.

These thoughts need to be replaced with the truth of God's word. Making the time to spend quietly in His presence, to study, and meditate upon it. As you do this, pray and ask the Lord to search your mind and heart for anything that is causing you fear.

The Holy Spirit will guide you in truth and give you the courage you need to let go of worry, doubt, insecurity, and any other form of fear. You cannot improve your circumstances by worrying; it only makes matters worse. Replacing a negative mindset with truth is needed to win the battle within your mind.

"And now, dear brothers and sisters, one final thing. Fix your thoughts on what is true, and honorable, and right, and pure, and lovely, and admirable. Think about things that are excellent and worthy of praise" (Phil. 4:8 NLT).

This does not mean that you have to deny the reality of a particular situation, but don't allow it to have power over you. When you allow yourself to be bogged down with thoughts of past hurts, sins, or the demands and decisions of daily life, you can easily lose your peace.

You can choose the direction of your thought life, whether they will be focused on the things of this world or the things of God (Col. 3:2).

"You will keep him in perfect peace, whose mind is stayed on You, because he trust in You" (Isa. 26:3).

Fix your mind on God & the way that:

- He has revealed Himself throughout time to His people.
- His ability to hold you up through His power.
- His ability to go before you and fight your battles.
- His provision and protection in a time of need.
- His ability to deal with your enemies effectively.

- His sacrifice of His only begotten Son to give you eternal life.

When it comes down to it, there is a choice to be made; continue to follow the enemy's advice and stay in bondage to fear or trust in the Lord and experience an abundant life and peace.

8 Living Victoriously

You have already obtained victory through the death of Jesus Christ on the cross, so you must refrain from a life of defeat and live victoriously. Walking in the authority and power of Jesus gives you victory. In addition, you need to maintain an intimate relationship with God through prayer and develop a thankful heart.

Prayer and Thankfulness

As with any other relationship, a greater sense of connection and intimacy is developed through communication. Yet, unlike any other relationship you have the opportunity to commune with the One who is all powerful and all knowing—through prayer. Prayer is a priority in the life of a believer. This special time with God should be sought after eagerly and consistently. The bible says we are to, "Devote yourselves to prayer, being watchful and thankful" (Col. 4:2).

Prayer leads you to dependence on God and relieves you of depending on yourself. You can confidently cast your cares on Him because of His infinite wisdom and everlasting love.

Casting your cares upon the Lord does not mean that you become indifferent regarding the situations you may encounter. You actively seek Him with the certainty that He will uphold you and give you peace in times of trouble.

Thankfulness is also needed to be victorious in this life. It is with thanks that you have the chance to honor God for who He is and all He does. Prayer and gratitude work together in the way that it quiets the doubts and fears within you. Prayer releases your cares upon Him and allows you to place your trust in God for whom nothing is impossible. Your thanks give God the praise and reverence He deserves as Creator and your loving Heavenly Father.

> Do not be anxious about anything, but in every situation, by prayer and petition, with thanksgiving, present your request to God. And the peace of God, which transcends all understanding, will guard your hearts and your mind in Christ Jesus.
>
> —Phil. 4:6-7 NIV

Prayer and gratitude allow your mind and heart to become aligned with God's will. As a result, you are better equipped to discern between the truth and the lies of the enemy.

Being strengthened through prayer, you exchange fear for courage and confidence that can only come from God. A consistent prayer life keeps you connected with God. Set aside special time everyday to spend with God in prayer. It does not matter what time of the day as long as you are able to focus on Him without distraction.

Remember that the quality of the time you spend in prayer is far more important than the quantity of time.

Firm in Faith

Even in times of uncertainty, you can be sure that God has a distinct purpose.

> Consider it pure joy, my brothers and sisters, whenever you face trials of many kinds, because you know that the testing of your faith produces perseverance. Let perseverance finish its work so that you may be mature and complete, not lacking anything.
>
> —James 1:2-4 NIV

Sometimes the difficulties you encounter serve as a way to develop you, molding you into a person of faith. In many cases your emotions can cause you to view circumstances from a negative perspective. It may even appear that God is not doing anything concerning your troubles. He may not work things out the way that you imagined, but it will definitely be in line with His purpose for your life. The way that God chooses to deliver you is entirely up to Him.

The troubles that you may face are often a way that God uses to demonstrate His power and be glorified through your life. When you allow yourself to rest in Him and stand firm in a time of fear you are letting His strength uphold you.

It is God's strength that will give you the ability to stand firm. His strength is made perfect in our weakness (2 Cor.12:9). The manner in which you choose to respond to things that evoke fear makes the difference. God gives you the grace that you need to endure in times of trouble. The best way to respond to your circumstances that bring about fear are through His promises. God has assured you throughout scripture that He will never forsake you. When you decide to stand firm in faith, you will have complete confidence in God and be fully persuaded that He is able to fulfill His word.

As a believer, you have been given authority through the power of Jesus Christ. It is not dependent on your ability, will power, or intellect. This authority works through the power of the Holy Spirit that dwells within. He is far greater than the enemy.

Abiding in Love

God's love is the source of strength and courage you need to live a victorious life. It is not enough for us to have a mere intellectual understanding of the love God has for you, but to experience a loving relationship with Him.

"And so we know and rely on the love God has for us. God is love. Whoever lives in love lives in God, and God in them." (1 John 4:16 NIV).

God desires for you to know Him and the depths of His love for His children. He understands our needs and sacrificed His only begotten Son in order for us to be reconciled to Him.

The devil wants you to remain in bondage and to continue to believe his lies. You are not considered unlovable, unequipped, unforgivable, nor do you have to feel inadequate. The truth is, the Lord is your source of strength when you feel weary, a faithful friend when you've been rejected, and the source of peace in troubled times.

Knowing God's immeasurable love starts with accepting His truth. Jesus said, "If you abide in My word, you are My disciples indeed. And you shall know the truth, and the truth shall make you free" (John 8:31-32).

When you know beyond a shadow of doubt that you have been accepted, equipped, and made righteous through Christ, then you can be sure God's love will drive out your fear.

Fear

One of the biggest obstacles for many Christians is allowing God's love to extend beyond the death of Christ at the cross. We know that He loved us enough to forgive our sins, but some may not realize that same love is a continual source to enrich every aspect of life.

You can always rely on God because He is unchanging. People can be fickle, but God has shown that He will not forsake us. Spiritual growth and effectiveness can be hindered when there is over-reliance on the opinions or approval of people. Although we live in a culture that encourages self-reliance, God desires for us to place our trust in Him and His love to sustain us. Many people, even some believers rely more on themselves, their resources, social status, education, achievements, or career to affirm them.

The desire for these things is not wrong in any way, but we must not allow the quest for them to overshadow God's love and our dependence on

Him. People-pleasing and self-reliance both lead to a state of constant performance.

The fear of rejection or preoccupation of the way others perceive you can interfere with the peace and contentment you should experience if you allow it. Choose to please God rather than man and let God deal with the outcome based on His perfect will for your life.

NOTES

NOTES

NOTES

NOTES

NOTES

NOTES

NOTES

NOTES

NOTES

Are you ready to boldly live the life

you were created for?

go to

www.TheWay2Victory.com